*Art and Culture*

# DESSERTS
## Around the World

**Comparing Fractions**

Monika Davies

## Consultants

**Michele Ogden, Ed.D**
Principal, Irvine Unified School District

**Jennifer Robertson, M.A.Ed.**
Teacher, Huntington Beach City School District

**Publishing Credits**
Rachelle Cracchiolo, M.S.Ed., *Publisher*
Conni Medina, M.A.Ed., *Managing Editor*
Dona Herweck Rice, *Series Developer*
Emily R. Smith, M.A.Ed., *Series Developer*
Diana Kenney, M.A.Ed., NBCT, *Content Director*
Stacy Monsman, M.A., *Editor*
Kevin Panter, *Graphic Designer*

**Image Credits:** p. 6 Interfoto/Alamy Stock Photo; p. 7 Chronicle/Alamy Stock Photo; p. 21 (top, middle, bottom) Sue Hwang; p. 23 Tim Hill/Alamy Stock Photo; all other images from iStock and/or Shutterstock.

**Teacher Created Materials**
5301 Oceanus Drive
Huntington Beach, CA 92649-1030
http://www.tcmpub.com

**ISBN 978-1-4807-5804-9**
© 2018 Teacher Created Materials, Inc.
Made in China
Nordica.022017.CA21700227

# Table of Contents

In a Chef's Shoes ..................................................... 4

America, Hungary, and Spain ............................. 6

Hong Kong and Brazil ......................................... 12

Turkey and Vietnam ............................................ 16

Poland and South Africa .................................... 20

Simple Mistake, Disgusting Dessert ................. 24

A Wide World of Food ........................................ 27

Problem Solving .................................................. 28

Glossary ............................................................... 30

Index ..................................................................... 31

Answer Key .......................................................... 32

# In a Chef's Shoes

People around the world enjoy the **culinary** arts. Some bake treats that tantalize your taste buds. Others make pastries with colors that catch your eye. But, there is one part of making sweet treats that everyone can agree on: every chef needs to use **fractions**!

Recipes are like road maps. They take people on tasty trips. Without a recipe, some chefs might end up lost. They would not know how much flour to use. They would not know which ingredients to add. Fractions are a part of many recipes. Chefs need to master them. Fractions help chefs make sure recipes are successes.

This biscuit recipe calls for fractional amounts of some ingredients.

There are hundreds of recipes for French macarons.

# America, Hungary, and Spain

Buckle up! Our road trip of world desserts begins now. The treats from the first three countries are baked to a golden brown.

## America's Chocolate Chip Cookies

Chocolate chip cookies are less than 100 years old. Their story began in the 1930s. That's when Ruth Graves Wakefield created America's favorite cookie. She owned a lodge called the Toll House Inn.

Wakefield's famous cookies were a lucky mistake. She was making cookies for her guests one day. But, she ran out of baker's chocolate. She looked through her shelves to find something she could use in its place. In the end, she cut up a chocolate bar. Ruth thought the pieces would melt. Instead, they stayed as chips! The chocolate chip cookie was born.

Ruth Graves Wakefield

Toll House Inn

## LET'S EXPLORE MATH

Fractions can be **compared** when the wholes are the same size and shape. Which of the examples can be used to compare fractions?

A.

B.

C.

D.

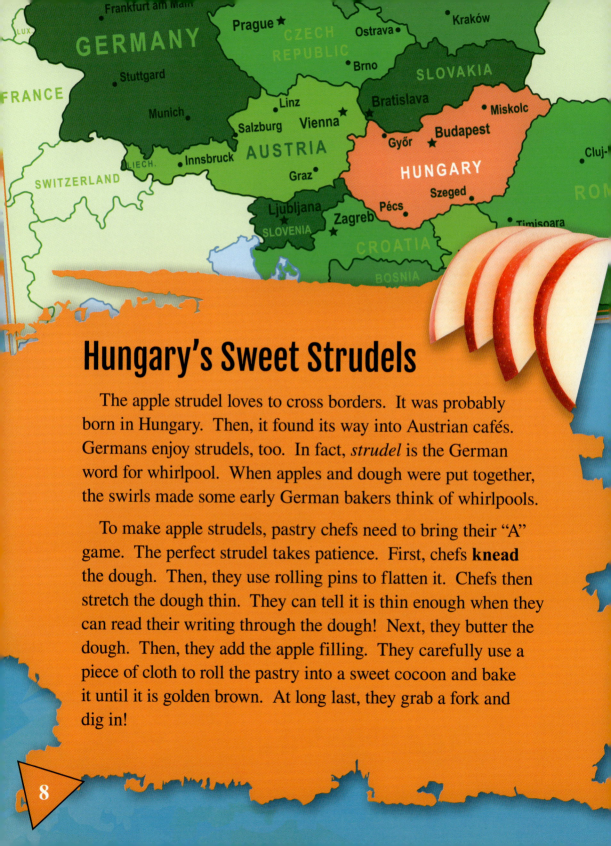

## Hungary's Sweet Strudels

The apple strudel loves to cross borders. It was probably born in Hungary. Then, it found its way into Austrian cafés. Germans enjoy strudels, too. In fact, *strudel* is the German word for whirlpool. When apples and dough were put together, the swirls made some early German bakers think of whirlpools.

To make apple strudels, pastry chefs need to bring their "A" game. The perfect strudel takes patience. First, chefs **knead** the dough. Then, they use rolling pins to flatten it. Chefs then stretch the dough thin. They can tell it is thin enough when they can read their writing through the dough! Next, they butter the dough. Then, they add the apple filling. They carefully use a piece of cloth to roll the pastry into a sweet cocoon and bake it until it is golden brown. At long last, they grab a fork and dig in!

A baker rolls an apple strudel into shape.

# Spain's Champion Churros

No one is sure who made the first churro. Some say Spanish shepherds were the first. They lived high up on hills and longed for a sweet treat. Churros would have been simple for them to fry. Others say sailors from Portugal traveled to China where they ate long doughnuts. The sailors took the idea back home. Their neighbors in Spain found out and gave the churro the star shape we know today.

The history of the churro may not be clear. But we do know that people love them. You can find them at American carnivals. Churros pop up on Spanish breakfast plates. They are filled with cream in Mexican bakeries. Churros have fans all around the world!

# Let's Explore Math

A pastry chef has customers who like desserts precut. Some buy only one small piece, while others want four or five. The chef needs to know which fractions are **equivalent** so prices can be fair. Use the number lines to answer the questions.

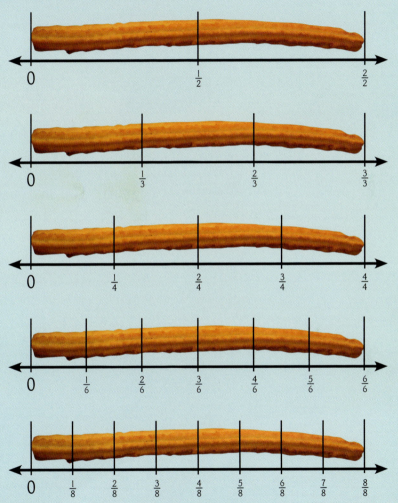

1. Which fractions are equivalent to $\frac{1}{2}$?
2. Which fractions are equivalent to $\frac{1}{3}$?
3. Which fractions are equivalent to $\frac{3}{4}$?

# Hong Kong and Brazil

What is something Hong Kong and Brazil have in common? Both share a love for desserts that are as bright as the sun!

## Hong Kong's Excellent Egg Tarts

Egg tarts are melt-in-your-mouth treats that are popular in Hong Kong. The recipe seems simple. The filling is made with water, eggs, sugar, and milk. Then, it is poured into pastry shells. Sounds easy, right? Not everyone thinks so.

It takes talent to make the perfect egg tart. The shell needs to have a **flaky** crust. The custard must be soft and not too sweet. Everything has to come together in a cheerful shade of yellow.

If that sounds complicated to you, you can leave the baking to a professional chef. If you can't jet over to Hong Kong, don't worry! You can find egg tarts in most Chinese bakeries.

# LET'S EXPLORE MATH

Imagine that a pastry chef in Hong Kong puts egg tarts in boxes. The chef also puts red cherries on some of the egg tarts.

1. Write a fraction for the number of egg tarts that have a red cherry.

2. Write a fraction for the number of egg tarts that do not have a cherry.

## Brazil's Quick Quindim

Do you have sugar, egg yolks, and milk in your kitchen? Then, you're nearly ready to start making quindim! And, you are well on your way to finding out why Brazilians love this **dense** dessert.

Quindim (keen-JEEN) is yellow and sweet. It is also easy to make. Even **novice** chefs can do it! First, chefs bring milk and sugar to a boil. They add egg yolks to give the treat a shiny glow. Then, melted butter and coconut go into the mix. Chefs pour the yellow mixture into molds. Lastly, they top it off with a final dose of sugar. Less than one hour later, quindim is served!

Quindim is usually served whole. Any whole number can be written as a fraction using one. One whole serving can be written as 1, or $\frac{1}{1}$. Or, 4 whole servings could be written as $\frac{4}{1}$.

## LET'S EXPLORE MATH

Rewrite the whole-number servings of quindim as fractions using 1.

1. 3 = _____
2. 8 = _____
3. 12 = _____

# Turkey and Vietnam

We are going green as we take a look at desserts in Turkey and Vietnam! Why green? Both countries offer gorgeous green desserts.

## Turkey's Bold Baklava

What is your favorite type of nut? Walnuts? Pistachios? Almonds? You have a choice when it comes to baklava (BAH-kluh-vah).

Turkey's beloved sweet is first made with phyllo (FEE-loh) dough. Phyllo has only two ingredients—water and flour. Each sheet of phyllo is stretched thinner than paper. Baklava needs 30 to 40 sheets of phyllo for one pastry!

The final steps are simple. Melted butter is brushed on each sheet. Then, it is time for that important choice of nut for the filling. Pistachios are the nut of choice that lend a shade of green to the treat. The final touch is a drizzle of honey. Then, you can dig your fork in and enjoy!

pistachios

baklava

## LET'S EXPLORE MATH

For the morning rush, a pair of Turkish chefs arrange rows of baklava. They **partition** each row into sections. Should all of the rows of baklava have the same price? Why or why not?

Pandan waffles are traditionally served plain, with no syrup or toppings.

## Vietnam's Wild Waffles

Have you ever wanted to try green eggs and ham? What about green waffles? You're in luck! Vietnam's bright-green pandan waffles are for you.

Why are they green? The color comes from the leaves of pandanus (pan-DAN-uhs) trees. These leaves are used in many Southeast Asian recipes. The trees are **native** to the area. Since they grow naturally here, the leaves are easy to get. They're also cheap. Some people even grow them at home.

The recipe also calls for coconut milk. Combining the milk and leaves together is key. This gives pandan waffles a sweet and nutty taste.

If you make these waffles, make sure you make a dozen. Everyone will want to try them!

# Poland and South Africa

The final part of our tour takes us to Poland and South Africa. Two of their famous desserts will change the way you think about bread and pudding.

babka

Raisins and cranberries are popular babka fillings.

# Poland's Beloved Babka

The word *babka* means "grandmother" in Polish. How did it get this name? It could be that the sides of the pan make swirls in the bread when it is baked. The swirls look like a grandmother's skirt. Or it could be that it is named after all the grandmothers who so often make it. In any case, many people call it delicious!

Babka bakers, on the other hand, might call it complicated. This sweet bread takes almost a whole day to make. Some recipes have more than 12 steps. Chefs start by cutting and rolling out the buttery dough. Usually, they fill it with raisins or fruit. They might even add chocolate or cinnamon. Then, they roll the dough into a long tube. Finally, they put the babka into a pan to bake. All of this work makes it a special treat for special times.

Babka dough is rolled flat.

The dough is rolled after filling is added.

The tube is placed in a pan for baking.

malva pudding

## South Africa's Popular Pudding

Do you think you know what pudding looks like? Malva pudding will likely be a surprise! This is not an American pudding in a cup. It is a cake! It has tart apricot jam on top. Many people love the hint of caramel. The cake also has some vinegar and baking soda in it. The two ingredients chemically react with each other and make small bubbles. The result is a **spongy** cake. Malva pudding is so soft that some call it marshmallow pudding.

Malva pudding is served in many restaurants in South Africa. Many people also bake it at home. Some chefs add chocolate or cherries. It might be served with custard, ice cream, or whipped cream. But, in any form, people can't get enough of malva pudding.

## LET'S EXPLORE MATH

Use the > or < symbols to show which fraction is greater:

1. Set A

   $\frac{1}{4}$ ___ $\frac{3}{4}$

   $\frac{4}{6}$ ___ $\frac{2}{6}$

   $\frac{6}{8}$ ___ $\frac{5}{8}$

2. Set B

   $\frac{2}{6}$ ___ $\frac{2}{3}$

   $\frac{1}{2}$ ___ $\frac{1}{8}$

   $\frac{3}{3}$ ___ $\frac{3}{4}$

3. Select one comparison from Set A and one comparison from Set B. Draw a picture to prove your solution to each.

Malva pudding is traditionally served hot with custard.

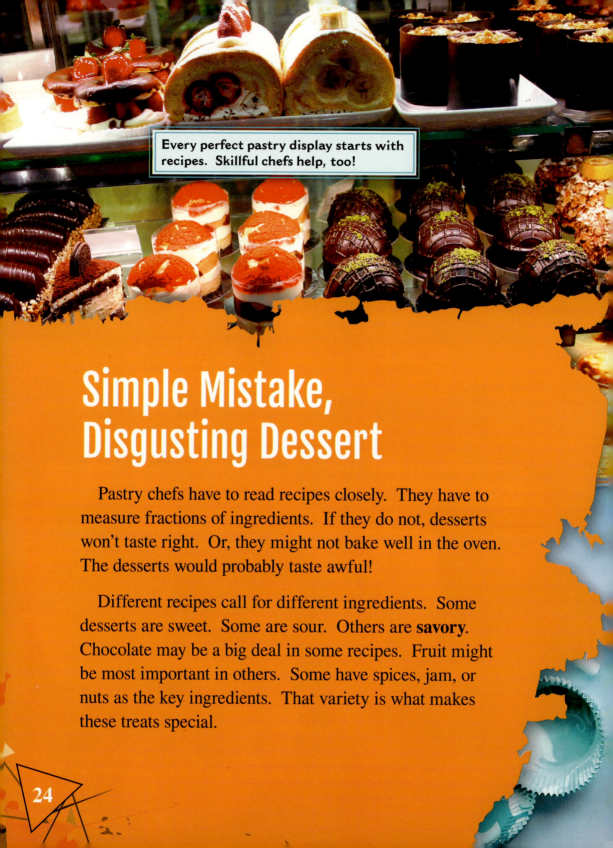

Every perfect pastry display starts with recipes. Skillful chefs help, too!

# Simple Mistake, Disgusting Dessert

Pastry chefs have to read recipes closely. They have to measure fractions of ingredients. If they do not, desserts won't taste right. Or, they might not bake well in the oven. The desserts would probably taste awful!

Different recipes call for different ingredients. Some desserts are sweet. Some are sour. Others are **savory**. Chocolate may be a big deal in some recipes. Fruit might be most important in others. Some have spices, jam, or nuts as the key ingredients. That variety is what makes these treats special.

## LET'S EXPLORE MATH

Butter and sugar appear in many dessert recipes but in different amounts. Use the partial recipes to answer the questions.

Churros: $\frac{1}{2}$ cup butter, $\frac{1}{4}$ cup sugar

Babka: $\frac{1}{4}$ cup butter, $\frac{1}{4}$ cup sugar

Chocolate chip cookies: 1 cup butter, $\frac{3}{4}$ cup sugar

1. Which dessert has more sugar: churros or chocolate chip cookies?
2. Which dessert has more butter: churros or babka?
3. Which dessert has an ingredient that could be written as $\frac{1}{1}$?

### Macaron Recipe

Ingredients:
* 3 egg whites
* $\frac{1}{4}$ cup white sugar
* $1\frac{2}{3}$ cups confectioners' sugar
* 1 cup finely ground almonds

Directions:
Line a baking sheet with a silicone baking mat. Beat egg whites in the bowl of a stand mixer fitted with a whisk attachment

# A Wide World of Food

Each country has its own **culture**. Food is part of that. People around the world enjoy special foods. Learning more about a culture can begin with recipes. Try some new food. Maybe try a dessert from this book! It's an easy way to get a taste of another country. You don't even have to leave home. Tasting new foods can introduce you to new favorites and help you learn about cultures other than your own.

Fractions can make or break a recipe. Chefs everywhere can agree on that. So, crack open a cookbook and let fractions lead the way.

## Churro Recipe

Ingredients:
* 1 cup water
* 2 tablespoons salt
* 2 tablespoons vegetable oil
* 1 cup all-purpose flour
* 2 quarts frying oil
* 1 cup white sugar
* 1 teaspoon cinnamon

Directions:
In a small saucepan over medi

# Problem Solving

Alisha and her dad are planning a family baking day. Alisha's favorite color is yellow. So, they decide to make quindim.

1. Alisha and her dad only have a $\frac{1}{4}$ cup measuring cup. How can they use this cup to measure the sugar and water?

2. Uh-oh! Alisha's dad made a mistake. He measured $\frac{1}{8}$ teaspoon of vanilla. Is that more or less than $\frac{1}{2}$ teaspoon of vanilla? Show your answer using the symbols > or <. How can he correct his mistake?

3. To make the recipe, each mold needs to be $\frac{3}{4}$ full. Alisha fills one mold $\frac{3}{4}$ full. Her dad fills the other mold $\frac{3}{8}$ full. Which mold has more batter? Use the symbols > or < to show your answer.

4. How can 6 egg yolks and 50 g shredded coconut be written as fractions?

## Quindim Recipe (makes 4)

2  250-milliliter baking molds and 1 pie dish

1 cup granulated sugar

$\frac{1}{2}$ cup water

50 g shredded coconut

1 tablespoon butter, melted

$\frac{1}{2}$ teaspoon vanilla

6 egg yolks

1. Preheat oven to 350°F (180°C).

2. Mix all ingredients in one bowl.

3. Grease molds with butter. Place molds into pie dish. Fill pie dish halfway with water.

4. Fill each mold $\frac{3}{4}$ full. Bake for 20 minutes.

5. Let quindim cool before eating. Enjoy!

# Glossary

**compared**—having looked at the features of two or more things

**culinary**—relating to or used in cooking

**culture**—the beliefs and ways of a group of people

**dense**—tightly compacted

**equivalent**—having the same number or value

**flaky**—breaks apart easily into smaller pieces

**fractions**—numbers that show how many equal parts are in wholes and how many of those parts are being described

**knead**—to use your hands to press

**native**—existing naturally in a certain area

**novice**—beginner

**partition**—divide into separate sections

**savory**—spicy or salty

**spongy**—soft and moist

# Index

America, 6, 10

babka, 20–21

baklava, 16–17

Brazil, 12, 14

chocolate chip cookie, 6

churro, 10

egg tarts, 12–13

Hong Kong, 12–13

Hungary, 6, 8

Malva pudding, 22–23

pandan waffles, 19

Poland, 20–21

quindim, 14–15, 28

South Africa, 20–22

Spain, 6, 10

strudel, 8–9

Turkey, 16

Vietnam, 16, 19

Wakefield, Ruth Graves, 6

# Answer Key

## Let's Explore Math

**page 7:**
A and D

**page 11:**
1. $\frac{2}{4}, \frac{3}{6}, \frac{4}{8}$
2. $\frac{2}{6}$
3. $\frac{6}{8}$

**page 13:**
1. $\frac{4}{6}$ or $\frac{2}{3}$
2. $\frac{2}{6}$ or $\frac{1}{3}$

**page 15:**
1. $\frac{3}{1}$
2. $\frac{8}{1}$
3. $\frac{12}{1}$

**page 17:**
Every row of baklava would cost the same because the wholes are the same.

**page 23:**
1. Set A: <, >, >
2. Set B: <, >, >
3. Answers will vary. Drawings should show equal-sized wholes partitioned into equal-sized pieces to make the comparison.

**page 25:**
1. chocolate chip cookies
2. churros
3. chocolate chip cookies; butter could be written as $\frac{1}{1}$

## Problem Solving

1. They can measure the sugar by using the $\frac{1}{4}$ measuring cup four times ($\frac{4}{4} = 1$ cup). They can measure the water by using the $\frac{1}{4}$ measuring cup twice ($\frac{2}{4} = \frac{1}{2}$ cup).
2. $\frac{1}{8} < \frac{1}{2}$. Alisha's dad can add 3 more $\frac{1}{8}$ teaspoons to correct his mistake. ($\frac{4}{8} = \frac{1}{2}$ teaspoon)
3. $\frac{3}{4} > \frac{3}{8}$
4. $\frac{6}{1}$ and $\frac{50}{1}$